Praise in the Valley of Despair

Praise in the Valley of Despair

A Book of Poems

by Carolyn Stovall

Xulon Press

Xulon Press
2301 Lucien Way #415
Maitland, FL 32751
407.339.4217
www.xulonpress.com

© 2020 by Carolyn Stovall

All rights reserved solely by the author. The author guarantees all contents are original and do not infringe upon the legal rights of any other person or work. No part of this book may be reproduced in any form without the permission of the author. The views expressed in this book are not necessarily those of the publisher.

Unless otherwise indicated, Scripture quotations taken from the King James Version (KJV) – *public domain.*

Printed in the United States of America.

ISBN-13: 978-1-6322-1639-7

Foreword

I am once again honored to say a word on behalf of my sister, Carolyn Stovall's work. This compilation of poems has been a comfort to me because of all the family and friends that we have recently lost, one after another.

God has given Carolyn strength to accomplish much for His people, even through cancer, death, family challenges, and severe pain. God uses Carolyn's poems to bring comfort, joy, peace, and strength when it is needed. They also make you think of your soul's worth to God. I believe you will enjoy this new set of poems as you allow them to minister to your heart.

Rita Kittrell
Sister in Christ and in the flesh

Acknowledgements

I would first like to acknowledge God who is the head of my life. It is he who has given me this gift by the power of the Holy Spirit. It is totally for His glory and to share with you. I would like to thank my husband Ted H Stovall, my family and friends. A special thanks to my mother for her encouragement and financial support, and to all those who donated time and money to make this book a success. Also, to my sister Rita Kittrell for her time and talent in the editing of this book.

I PRAY THAT ALL WHO READ THIS BOOK WILL BE BLESSED.

Preface

I have had the privilege of being one of God's chosen vessels to pour forth His love, His comfort, and His peace through this book, Praise in the Valley of Despair.

You will thoroughly be encouraged as you read this anointed book.

Praise in the Valley of Despair takes you on life's journey from despair to hope and faith in Christ Jesus our Saviour.

The simplicity of this book and the truths unveiled can turn your heart towards God and enrich your life.

Table of Contents

Foreword vii
Acknowledgements ix
Preface xi

Valley of Grief and Loss 1

   A Job Well Done 2
   A Knitted Friendship 3
   Affected 4
   An Appointed Time 5
   Completed Purpose 6
   Could Have Been 7
   Death's Appointment 9
   Finally 10
   God Saw Fit 11
   Grown Apart 12
   Home Going 13
   I Can Still Hear You 14
   Knocking at the Door 15
   No Blame, No Shame 16
   Precious Saints 17
   Remember Your Mother's Love 18
   Sacrificial Altar 19

The Trial Not Chosen........................... 20
Truly God Knows 21
When Day Is Done............................. 22
When the Battle Is Over 23
You Left 25

Valley of Pain and Suffering 27

A Kinship with Cancer 29
A Night In Hell 30
A Plan and a Purpose 31
God Is Still a Healer 32
God Knows My Trial 33
God Thought Me Worthy To Suffer.............. 34
I Thought About My Friend.................... 35
I Thought It Was a Death Sentence 36
Learning to Trust 38
Suffering To Glorify God 39
Welcomed, Not Dreaded....................... 40
Who Really Understands 41
You Must Go Through......................... 42
Your Vessel To Use............................. 43

Valley of Restoration and Salvation............... 45

Be Truthful.....................................47
Beginnings 48

Chosen, Holy, and Acceptable.................... 49
Could You Not Watch One Hour 50
Covered.. 52
Created, Called, and Forgiven.................... 53
Gradual Straying 54
Grandma's Prayers.............................. 55
Have Mercy With Me, Jesus...................... 56
He's Got the Whole World in His Hands......... 57
If This Were Your Last Day...................... 58
My Calling 60
The Thief's Last Words 61
The Soul's Worth 62
Understood.................................... 63
Undeserving................................... 64
Unforgiveness or Freedom 65
Wake-Up Call.................................. 66
We Are All On Our Way........................ 67
Why Do I Make You So Small, God?............ 68

Valley of Encouragement........................ 69

A Servant's Clothes............................. 71
Accepted 72
Broken But Useable 73
Dark Night of the Soul 74
Go the Extra Mile............................... 76

He Leads The Way 77
In His Presence 78
Jesus Loves Even Me. 79
Journey to the Crown. 80
Joy. 81
Man of God 82
Suffer the Children. 83
The Influence of a Mother. 84
You Are God's Light 86

About the Author **87**

Valley of Grief and Loss

In the Valley of Grief and Loss we find that we must make the journey there. Grief and loss are some things we will experience, whether because of a death, health issues, divorce, financial or relationship problems. There will be times that you feel that your heart is breaking, and pain never seems to subside. I want you to know that here we can find God's grace and peace, no matter what we go through. He is the great comforter.

On this journey, we will learn to trust in the Lord our Savior. We will also learn that He is in your trial with you. He bears part of your burden and carries you when you are weak. It is here where we learn to pray, not selfishly, but to seek the Lord's face. We become real with God. We take off the mask and bare our souls. Be assured that here we learn that God will bring us through the trial, and we will see light at the end of the journey. For He is waiting for you to trust Him.

A Job Well Done

This is the day that God is glorified
When He says a job well done
He has sent His only begotten son, Jesus
To usher in His precious ones

The angels in heaven are rejoicing
The heavenly gates are open wide
You get to walk down the golden streets
With Jesus right by your side

You get to say Hallelujah to the Lamb
That was slain for you and me
Who shed His blood and washed us clean
So we could enter Eternity

Your work on earth is over
Your purpose is now complete
Come rest from your toils and labor
And sit at the Savior's feet

A Knitted Friendship

I thought about us growing up
When we used to laugh and play
We attended church on a regular basis
That included all day on Sunday

We went off on our separate journeys
For college we were bound
And somewhere our paths crossed again
One another we both have found

We knew that it was God alone
Who knitted our friendship together
We have stood the test of time
Many storms of life we've weathered

And now the Lord has seen fit
For we knew it would one day come
Yes, heaven's gates are open wide
Jesus will now usher in His dear son

It was God alone who sustained us
And knitted our hearts together in love
We now have our precious memories
Until we also meet the Father above

Affected

I feel that I must tell you
I know you do not know
Just how your leaving affected us
When you left a long time ago

At first I was very hopeful
That one day you would appear
The longer you stayed away, Dad
I developed anxiety, shame, and fear

Sleepless nights, they came and haunted me
I pray both night and day
For God to bring you back to me
Somehow, somewhere, someday

But time began to pass away
And years began to fade
Life was very hard for me
But we made it, Dad, someway

I saw Mommy on her knees
I never saw her cry
She prayed and asked for help from God
His grace and mercy He supplies

An Appointed Time

Everyday someone is dying
Some are young and some are old
Some we are surprised at
And some we wish they would hurry up and go

Some are very fearful
And they fight hard to remain here
They try out every solution to stay
For their life is very dear

Some are relieved and willing
For they know Christ as Savior and Lord
And He will usher them into His kingdom
And their blessings will be restored

Some are peaceful even in suffering
They're not grumpy, not at all
But resting in God's promises
And listening for His call

So, no matter where you are in life
It doesn't matter if you are rich or poor
There is an appointed time for us all
He will one day knock on your heart's door

Completed Purpose

The Lord saw fit to take you
Your purpose is now complete
You can gather around His Throne
And sit at your Savior's feet

No more suffering and sorrow
This old life is gone away
You have a new home in glory
That you can walk around in today

You can worship and praise the Lord Jesus
He shed His blood and died for you
He intercedes at the right hand of the Father
He bought redemption, salvation, and sanctification, too

The tears we cry are of joy
As we remember your sacrifice of love
But Jesus loved you more than us
He has ushered you to heaven above

Could Have Been

We could have been a powerful ministry
A vessel for God to use
To reach the world for Salvation
To spread the message, the "Good News"

But somehow things didn't turn out
The way I thought that they would
It's been a journey of solitude
Things didn't turn out so good

Just me and God together
I've been so all alone
We didn't discuss the Bible
Or pray when we were home

And yet I must keep on going
For God calls me everyday
To do His will and not my will
To humble myself and pray

To give up all my hopes and dreams
And place them at His feet
As a sacrificial offering
Humility to God is sweet

continued

So I trust you, God, in whatever

The things that You must do
I offer myself as an offering
That I may bring glory alone to You

Death's Appointment

Death is a sad occasion
And we wish that you were still here
We ask so many questions, "Why?"
And some have even cried tears

The sorrow, pain, and grief
And words we did not say
You must now release it to Jesus
For I have now gone far away

We know this is God's plan for you
For your work on earth is done
And we, too, have an appointed time
And it will one day come

We must get our house in order
For we don't know how or when
We all have an appointment with death
To meet Jesus when He calls for you my friend

Finally

Now I can finally see the King
To be ushered to His throne
To bow at the feet of Jesus
My king, my redeemer, my own

I know I have left my loved ones here
But this date has been set for me
Please, my love, wipe away the tears
I can finally say I am free

There is no sickness or pain here
No sorrow or suffering for me
I have finally met Jesus my Savior
For now, I fulfilled my destiny

Now yes, your heart is broken in two
You are lonely and your mind is confused
Let Jesus comfort you in your grief, my child
It is only He who can carry you through

God Saw Fit

I cannot handle the hurt
The pain is too great to bear
I know you will be with Jesus
For He alone doth care

He saw fit for you to suffer
He chose this trial for you
Suffering is a part of the cross
But the Lord will carry you through

I know that you will be with Him
For heaven will now be your home
For He will come to usher you in
The Lord will not leave you here alone

So, I promise to take comfort
In the Word of God, it's true
And God will give me the peace I need
As I glorify Him, for I know I must go through

Grown Apart

My heart is a little heavy
And my eyes filled with tears
Of all the time we spent together
Which were a lot of years

But now I see a difference
Where we have grown apart
And I can grieve the sadness
Which has plagued my little heart

I am reminded of Jonathan and David
Their love remains the same
And yes, they made a covenant
They were bound in Jesus's name

So now friend I will pray for you
On this journey you must make
And we will learn many lessons
For our Lord makes no mistakes

Home Going

Surely, we are going to miss you
And there is grief that we will bear
By trusting in our Savior and Lord
We will make it because Jesus cares

You have been committed to God's faithful work
And your purpose here now is complete
God has come to bring you home
You deserve to sit at the Savior's feet

Now your mansion in heaven is ready
We must now release you, my dear
God's love now completely surrounds us
And we have nothing now to fear

Our memories will never fade
And we, too, will one day meet
Jesus our Lord and Savior
Around the throne we will sit at His feet

I Can Still Hear You

When I can't talk, pray for me
Talk to me for I can hear
It helps me pass through
For my Savior God is near

I've cherished His Word
Read it to me everyday
The Psalms bring me great comfort
Cheers my heart in some kind of way

His Word reminds me that He loves me
And He is coming very soon
He will usher me into His kingdom
Could be morning, night, or noon

My work on earth is completed
I have glorified the Son
I have a home in glory
For the battle now is won

Knocking at the Door

You heard the knocking at the door
And there is no need to fear
Know that our heavenly Father is calling you
And He is always near

He sometimes gives you warning
That your purpose on earth is complete
And that soon He plans to come for you
For the Savior you are soon to meet

He knows you have your family ties
And the beautiful children you will leave
They will have wonderful memories
Now you get to see Jesus,
the one who died for you and me

No Blame, No Shame

Don't blame yourself
Don't second guess
The things you should
Or should not do.
Remember our days are ordained by God
Surrender these thoughts
And pray your way through

Know that I have loved you
We were a great family
You've been a wonderful
Husband, father and friend
God will never take these memories
Away from thee.

Precious Saints

Precious in the sight of the Lord is the death of one of
His saints
Psalm 116:15

I know it's hard to understand
With this carnal mind we have
God says the death of a saint is precious
Yet we all are quite so sad

When we look at trials and tribulations
And suffering we all have gone through
God has promised us eternal life
Salvation is a free gift for you

There is a home in glory
When your work on earth is complete
He says now rest from all your labor
Your heavenly Father is waiting for you to meet

Remember Your Mother's Love

If tomorrow I were to leave you
And go to the Father above
Continue to be obedient children
And remember your mother's love

Continue to help your father
In any way that you can
Continue to cheer him up with your love
For he will be a lonely man

Continue to serve the Lord
Making Him the center of your life
Continue to be humble and pray
For Jesus to remove all bitterness and strife

Continue to share God's love
With everyone that you see
Forgiving those who do wrong to you
And accepting humility

Continue to accept the things
Which God has prepared for thee
Remember your mother will love you
For all eternity

Sacrificial Altar

I lay my feeling upon the altar
In the quietness of my little heart
At any given moment, Lord
The tears may right now start

I am really having a struggle, Lord
But I know what I must do
I guess I've carried it far too long
Here at the altar I give it to You

I know that the Holy Spirit
Will give me the peace I need
Comfort my little heart, dear Lord
Please forgive my anxiety

The Trial Not Chosen

This is not the trial we would have chosen
For it literally tore our family apart
Even though there was love and understanding
So much grief played havoc on our hearts

It brought us to our knees daily
Seeking God's will in all this distress
Not knowing from day to day
How we are going to get out of this mess

We've tried to love unconditionally
Just as Jesus requires us to do
At times we didn't know if we were going to make it
Just how was our family going to get through?

God says all things will work together
For those who truly believe
Jesus is far greater than ever
Trusting Him for His blessing to receive

So, we want to encourage you on your journey
Wherever the Holy Spirit leads you
Jesus is standing in the midst of this trial
Bearing the burden, for He is faithful and true

Truly God Knows

I cannot imagine the sadness
Or the pain that you must bear
I want you to know that the Savior
He loves you and He cares

And yes, your heart is heavy
Yes, tears may fill your eyes
I know that God will help you
You can trust Him as days pass by

Dear friend, I know He loves you
And God will carry you on through
When you think you cannot make it
God knows what's best to do

When Day Is Done

When my day is done
And my purpose is complete
I will rest from my labor
And sit at my Savior's feet

I will mourn no more
With suffering or pain
But sing out the praises of Jesus
In heaven's choirs I will sing

I will receive the rewards
For all the work which I did
And receive payment for a life
On earth for the Savior which I lived
So, when day is done
And He calls me home
My Jesus I will see
The one who hung on that old rugged cross
He did it just for me

And when your mission is over
God's plan is now complete
You may now rest from your labor
And sit at the Savior's feet

When the Battle Is Over

Hear ye, hear ye, children of the Lord
For when the battle is over
I shall wear a crown
I shall wear a crown
I shall wear a golden crown

Once again, we celebrate
How the Lord has brought us through
It's by His grace and mercy
And nothing we could ever do

It's only because He loves us
That He sent His son to die
And gave us His Holy Spirit
Salvation is the reason why

He brought us through some dark times
When we look back over our past
We can ring the bell of freedom
Thank God we are free at last

But God, He has displeasure
In the things we do and say
We do not know Him personally
And some have slipped away

continued

We have a form of worship
Attending church may be a part
Other things are more important
God's not first and sin is in your heart

It's only when you are struggling
That you seek Him night and day
You have the pure audacity
To get on your knees and pray

You rarely read the Word of God
Other things are more important to you
But there will be a judgment
On the things you say and do

God wants you to know, church
That the journey is not complete
You cannot afford to do nothing
And try to sit at the Savior's feet

He has given us a job
For there is so much work to be done
Only then can we proclaim
That the victory has been won

You Left

We looked up to you
You were mighty and strong
We never saw your failures
Or the things that you did wrong

You had this big loud voice
That could shake the mountains tall
And eyes that could penetrate
Even me yet being oh so small

Your words were free and mighty
You meant just what you said
You didn't raise your voice
When you said, "It's time for bed."

And yes, you were my hero
I wanted to be just like you
And then one day you went away
What was this child to do?

I cried and cried for many days
Sleepless nights they did creep in
For you did not understand my loss
A child's love never ends

Valley of Pain and Suffering

On our journey through the Valley of Pain and Suffering, we experience God's grace and mercy. Here we learn a valuable lesson: to wait on the Lord's timing and develop peace in the midst of the storm. We know that, in the beginning, God created a perfect world where there was no pain and suffering. When Adam and Eve sinned by disobeying the commands of God, this unleashed pain that they never experienced before. Their eyes were opened to good and evil.

God killed the first animal sacrifice, the spotless Lamb of God, to clothe them. He expelled them from the garden. Here they experienced not only physical pain, but also spiritual pain. They were forever separated from God. They were no longer able to walk with Him in the cool of the day or enjoy face-to-face communication with God. Greater suffering came when their firstborn son Cain murdered his brother, Abel.

Henceforth, little children and adults experienced insurmountable pain and suffering. Jesus our Lord told us in the Word of God that we, too, will suffer pain, but be of good cheer—He has overcome the world. He is acquainted with all of our pain, for He himself bore our pain on the cross. He died that we might have life and overcome the attacks of the enemy, Satan. Yes, we find hope and joy in the midst of our pain all because of Christ Jesus our Lord.

A Kinship with Cancer

Because I have this Cancer
I've found a kinship everywhere
I am the Lord's witness
There is hope and, yes, He cares

Some days may be a struggle
Racked with pain and suffering
I've cried a river of tears
Wondering what this Cancer can bring

Sometimes you lose your focus
And chemo fog clouds your mind
You feel a sense of hopelessness
And peace you cannot find

Your friends and family are worried
For they don't know what to do
And they feel a sense of helplessness
They don't know how to help you

I want you to know the Lord
He can be with you everyday
You must trust and lean on Him
Seek the Lord and let Jesus have His way

A Night In Hell

I understand that suffering comes
To everything in the land
It is a part of the original sin
From the curse God put on man

Many times, we ask the question, Why?
What have I done wrong?
The pain is so excruciating
And you cry, My Lord, how long?

Way up high in the heavens
Satan challenged God to a test
To remove His divine hand from upon you
That you would curse God and not confess

You have tried to walk in holiness
Doing the things you know are right
You cannot understand what's happening
Tears flow morning, noon, and night

But God, He knows your character
He knows what you will do
He knows that you will trust Him
And He will bring you through

A Plan and a Purpose

I understand that suffering comes
To everything in the land
It is a part of the original sin
From the curse God put on man

When I heard that I had Cancer
I was not shocked at all
I was not sad or angry
But on Jesus I did call

I knew there was a purpose
I knew God had a plan
He chose me to be His vessel
To bring hope throughout the land

He gave me peace and comfort
And never once did I fear
For I knew my Lord and Savior
Was not far away but near

Daily my Lord and Savior
Has put a smile upon my face
He gives grace and mercy
As I run this Cancer race

God Is Still a Healer

I'm trusting God for your healing
And praying for you every day
God has a special assignment for you
You must let him have His way

At times you may be discouraged
And you do not understand
Draw closer to the Lord our God
He will strengthen your inner man

Your outer man may suffer much
And at times you just don't know
God will give you strength, my child
He will lead you where you must go

He will never leave or forsake you, child
He is in this trial with you
One day the Lord will bring you out
You will testify what the Lord our God can do

God Knows My Trial

Jesus knows what you have gone through
He has allowed this trial for you
He is waiting for you to trust Him
The Lord knows you can make it through

On this journey there were decisions
Some were good and some were bad
Some wrecked the core of your very being
Feeling God's grace, you never had

But through it all, He's blessed you
He has carried this cross each day
He has you by His grace, my child
So you won't be led astray

So, in this trial, just trust Him
There is a reward for you at the end
For joy will come in the morning
If you keep trusting God, my friend

God Thought Me Worthy To Suffer

God thought me worthy to suffer for Him
To bear the sin and shame
Rejected and hurt by many
Who never even knew my name

God thought me worthy to suffer
So He gave Satan permission
To test me to the limit
Sometimes through terrible conditions

God thought me worthy to suffer
Knowing He was always near
He gave me grace abundantly
And wiped away all of my tears

God thought me worthy to suffer
Knowing the battle had been won
Through the death, burial, and resurrection of Christ
The victory is through Jesus Christ, God's precious son

I Thought About My Friend

I thought about my friend
As tears welled up inside
And I saw how the love of God
In the innocence of life abides

She found me pure and simple
As she threw her arms around me
She showered me with love and kisses
Very unconditionally

She would ask me how I was feeling
Did I have any pain at all?
Purely concerned about my welfare
For on Jesus did we call

He knew all the pain and suffering
On the cross He died for me
He knew when I got to heaven
My spirit would be free

So, I ask you, Lord, to bless her
Keep her on her knees to pray
Fill her again with your Spirit
As she intercedes today

I Thought It Was a Death Sentence

When I heard the word Cancer
A million things ran through my mind
What kind do I have? Where is it located?
Has it been there a very long time?

Then my mind was flooded
A rush of feeling pushed right in
And gripped my mind with emotions
I can't remember all of them

At first there was fear and panic
What in the world was I going to do?
I was in a state of shock
Upon hearing my bad news

Then I felt warm tears
Streaming from my eyes
As I thought that I might not make it
That I might even die

I heard a still small voice
Trust me, child, I am here
I will be with you on this journey
So, there is no need to fear

There will be some bumpy roads ahead
And you will feel sometimes alone
Pain will attack your body, my child
Remember, I made your heart my home

So, nothing that you will go through
My child, can I not understand
For I bear the scars from Calvary
And the nail prints in my feet and hands

Learning to Trust

You deserve the glory and honor
All praise is due Your name
If we put our trust in Jesus
We will never ever be the same

He is right there working it out
He is doing what's best for you
You might not even understand
All the wonderful things our God can do

So, in the midst of trials, just trust Him
For He has the master plan
When He feels you've learned your lessons
He'll snatch you out of the enemy's hands

Suffering To Glorify God

I cannot handle the hurt
The pain is too great to bear
I know you will be with Jesus
For He alone doth care

He has saw fit for you to suffer
He chose this trial for you
Suffering is a part of the cross
But the Lord will carry you through

I know that you will be with Him
For heaven will be your home
For He will come to usher you there
The Lord will not leave you alone

So, I promise to take comfort
In the Word of God, it is true
And God will give me the peace I need
As you glorify Him in the trial facing you

Welcomed, Not Dreaded

I don't dread that I have Cancer
It's a different world, you see
I get to minister to God's children
As they minister to me

I have so many lessons
That I have learned along the way
It has forced me to seek my Savior
I have humbly bowed and prayed

I have seen many suffering
Some are angry, some are sad
Some have even cursed my God
They are hurting and, yes, very mad

They do not understand
Life is a journey, one we must all take
We are enslaved by our humanness
Yes, we all will make mistakes

God can help you if you trust Him
He can give His comfort and peace
He can bring hope in the midst of despair
And your soul can find release

Who Really Understands

It doesn't seem to get better
You feel that there is no way out
Physical pain can make you crazy
"Who understands me?" are the words you shout

Your family, yes, they get tired
And friends now only a few
The TV becomes your best friend
You turn it on to hear only the news

Now your children you scarcely see
They have their own lives, you say
They haven't the time to make it here
They may come to see you one day

You Must Go Through

It's not that I cannot deliver you
But you must go through this trial
It might seem like it will last forever
But it will be there for a little while

Although I have forgiven you
And cleansed your heart from sin
You must work out your own salvation
This is where real faith begins

You must learn to trust God daily
"Though He slay me," I will say:
Have your way with me Lord
I surrender my will today

I have to learn to trust you
With both the good and the bad
To glorify Your holy name
Even if I hurt and feel sad

I know that suffering and sorrow
Are part of the cross that I must bear
But you have promised to go with me
And grace and mercy will be right there

Your Vessel To Use

Oh God, I am grateful how You blessed me
You have given me oh so much
For You have used me as Your vessel
And my heart, Lord, You have touched

You have led me to the valley of despair
Where I found no relief
Just tears of pain and suffering
I am overcome, alone with grief

But here, where I am broken
My soul cries night and day
I cry out and surrender
Lord, I will let You have Your way

Valley of Restoration and Salvation

In this valley, God restores. He builds your trust, your faith, and your hope through the many trials that you have gone through. God says in His Word, "I will never leave thee or forsake thee" (Heb.13:5). What a magnificent promise for us to hold onto. He also says that "God is not a man, that he should lie; neither the son of man, that he should repent: hath he said, and shall he not do it? Or hath he spoken, and shall he not make good (Num. 23:19). So, with this promise, no matter what you go through, hold on by faith. For God is faithful.

In regard to salvation, in this valley you can praise God who hath provided a way out for us. Salvation belongs to God. For it is through the pain and suffering that He is glorified when we praise Him. I am reminded of Paul and Silas, beaten and wrongfully thrown into prison, and yet they praised God and sang songs. At the appointed time, God released them. So, we learn to find joy in the midst of the trial. Our joy is that, no matter what we go through, we have the joy of our salvation and eternal life. The Word says, "Though He slay me, yet will I trust Him (Job 13:15). Words that come to mind I heard a long time ago, must Jesus bear the cross alone and all the world go free. Yes, there is a cross for Jesus, and there is a cross for me.

Be Truthful

When you have been devastated in your dealings
And your character is considered flawed
Know that you won't get away with it
There will be some testing sent from God

You may find yourself in trouble
And you don't know what to do
You must seek the Lord your God
He has a lesson prepared for you

You must prove yourself to be trustworthy
God looks at the intent of the heart
He wants only to forgive you
To cleanse and give you a fresh new start

So, I challenge you to surrender
Let the Holy Spirit have His way
God will exchange it for Salvation
You must be truthful in every way

Beginnings

In the beginning, GOD
Created the world and the heavens
And all that lies therein
He put a plan of redemption in place
For He knew that we would sin

He knew He would come in a body
Wrapped in flesh and blood
One day He would give His life
For the people that He loved

God demonstrated how much He loved us
For He died on Calvary
So that the people He created
Would worship Him freely

He gave the gift of choice
He wanted a willing worker's heart
To trust Him in the midst of things
Because of love, they would never part

So, in the beginning, GOD created everything
Now we can again have fellowship everyday with Him
And we can bring an offering of thanksgiving and praise
Glorifying God's holy name, my friend

Chosen, Holy, and Acceptable

God has chosen you, beloved
To be a child of the King
To spread forth His love and mercy
And His praises every day to sing

He has chosen you and ordained you
Before the foundation of the world
And offered free salvation
To every woman, man, boy, and girl

He forgave you of your sins
And set you free within
By His blood and cleansing power,
Resurrection and life begin

You are a child of the King
Holy, acceptable, and now set apart
Sealed by the Holy Spirit and grace
So, let nothing defile your little heart

Could You Not Watch One Hour

And he cometh unto his disciples, and findeth them asleep, and saith unto Peter, What, could ye not watch with me one hour? Watch and pray, that ye enter not into temptation: the spirit indeed is willing, but the flesh is weak.

(Matthew 26:40, 41)

Can you imagine the disappointment of Jesus
When He found the disciples asleep
While He stretched out prostrate before His Father
Pouring out His soul, tears of blood He did weep

It was the valley of the shadow of death
All alone He prayed and cried
Surrendering up His total will
Knowing soon He would be crucified

It was history's greatest betrayal
Not one disciple stood by His side
Denying that they never knew Him
They ran away in fear to hide

But He still loved and cared for them
He knew all along what they would do
Jesus forgave and He also restored them
Knowing Salvation would cleanse and make them new

He hung on the cross and died
In three days, Jesus arose from the grave
He broke the chains of death and sin
And now the world could be saved

Covered

Yielded and surrendered
My will is not my own
I have given my life to Jesus
He has made my heart His home

He has changed my heart within
I will never ever be the same
He has stamped His seal of approval
I am covered by His name

My sins have been covered by His blood
He has washed and made me new
He has put His spirit inside my heart
I don't want to do the things I used to do

I am totally committed to Christ my Lord
It's no longer I who lives, but it is He
And the life I now live, I live by faith
No more bondage, no more guilt, I am free

Created, Called, and Forgiven

You desire truth in the inner-most part
For You alone know I have sinned
I tried to cover up a lie
But You exposed the sin within

I fell into temptation
A trap laid carefully for me
I did not expect You to uncover
The sin that covered me

Lord, today I must confess
So that my spirit can be free
To break the yolk of slavery
By Your Spirit please wash and forgive me

Gradual Straying

When things are going well in our lives
And blessings are flowing our way
We tend to be complacent with God
In the things we do and say

We speak more of the secular things
And fail to see how He provides
Negative things become our focus
We become self-centered and walk in our own pride

But God He does not like it
He will uncover all of your sins
He wants you totally committed
And for you to lean on Him

He will take His covering from you
And He will let you stray away
Until you truly seek Him out
And repent, then He will change your ways

Grandma's Prayers

Grandma's words ring in my ear
To do things that are right
It doesn't matter who is watching you
You are always in God's sight

She took me to church to hear the Word of God
In my heart she prayed for it to be instilled
That I would surrender to Jesus
And to do His perfect will

At times I made wrong choices
I began to stray away
I want you to know that my grandmother
Stayed on her knees and prayed

By His grace and tender mercies
He chastened me back to the right path
When I accepted Jesus as my personal Savior
Her prayers were answered at last

Have Mercy With Me, Jesus

Have mercy with me, Jesus
I am crying out to You
Have mercy with me, Jesus
For I don't know what to do

Have mercy with me, Jesus
Lord, please don't let me stray
Have mercy with me, Jesus
Lord, I am yielding to You today

Have mercy with me, Jesus
Lord, teach me how to obey
Have mercy with me, Jesus
Lord, please show me the right way

Have mercy with me, Jesus
Pick me up, Lord, when I fall
Have mercy with me, Jesus
Lord, please don't let me miss Your call

Have mercy with me, Jesus
Lord, please let me do Your will
Have mercy with me, Jesus
As You teach me to be still

He's Got the Whole World in His Hands

Remember the song, which is very true
He's got the whole world in His hands
It is He who brings things into existence
It's not the invention of mere man

He controls the seasons
Everything that you can see
God is God alone and lives
And has a destiny for thee

You were created with a purpose
To give glory to His name
To praise Him for the work He's done
Salvation you will gain

Confess your sins to Jesus
Commit your life to Him
You will never be disappointed
His Spirit will live within

If This Were Your Last Day

If this were your last day
What would you do?
Would you be upset and cry
Or praise your way through?

Would you trust in the Savior
For His peace of mind?
Would you reconcile differences
That have been stewing for a very long time?

Would you help the poor stranger
And the people that you've met?
Would you forgive those
Who have entered into your debt?

Would you go out of your way
To be especially kind?
Doing more for others
With the people that you find?

Would you share God's grace and mercy
And tell how His blood washes away sin?
That His free gift of salvation
Will bring new life within?

Would you take comfort in knowing?
His eternal life is given free
And you will have a home in glory
That has been prepared especially for thee

My Calling

I don't expect you to understand
My calling of the Lord
Nor what He chose for me to do
Or how the Savior did restore

He picked me up out of the depths of sin
He placed His Spirit inside
And He told me that He loved me
In my heart He would reside

He set me on a course
This journey I am on today
He told me to always remember
That He is the Truth, the Light, the only Way

So even when I stumble and fall
Into the pit of sin
I know that I can go to God
And confess my sin to Him

He is faithful to forgive
And cleanses me everyday
I know that my Heavenly Father
Will not take His Spirit away

The Thief's Last Words

Remember me were the words of the thief
That hung on the cross nearby
He saw Jesus as the Son of God
And He humbled Himself before he died

This crime I have committed, Lord,
And punishment I am due
But the son of God did nothing wrong
And Calvary's cross isn't for you

Remember me were the words of the thief
When you enter your kingdom upon high
Forgive me for the wrong I did
A repentant heart cries out inside

Please cleanse my heart within, dear Lord
By washing me in thy blood
Remember me were his words
When you go to the Father above

The Soul's Worth

You can always make money
It soon brings an emptiness inside
You can have cars and material things
But peace is eluded inside

You can rise up the corporate ladder
You can be proud of the things you've done
But if you do not have a relationship with Jesus
Your fall has just begun

You must want Him more than these things
Your heart has to be broken into
You must surrender your will to Jesus
So His Spirit can work with you

He will give you the peace you long for
You will learn to have joy in the midst of pain
Suffering is the way of the cross
But you really have much to gain

Please, trust the Lord your God
To complete His work in you
When you finally surrender to Jesus
His work can begin anew

Understood

You said you understood
And you listened very well
But the problem has some deep dark roots
In the heart yes, I can tell

I see bitterness and strife
Unforgiveness dwells inside
Some jealousy may appear
These things you just can't hide

You strike quick as a snake
Poisonous venom you leave there
I know you are hurting badly
But anger shows up everywhere

I will pray for you continuously
For deliverance soon to come
Only Jesus can help you, friend
For His restoration to be done

Undeserving

You do not judge me now
Since God has changed my heart
He forgave me of my sins
And gave me a brand-new start

He surrounded me with His love
And shed His grace upon me
He says I no longer am the same
That He has set me free

While others did condemn me
I know that I am new
His mercy undeserving
I now have much work to do

To testify of His goodness
So others just might see
When I confessed my sin to Jesus
He restored and gave eternal life to me

Unforgiveness or Freedom

Oh, yes, you really hurt me
And I plotted my revenge
I would never forgive you
Though I knew that this was sin

I thought you changed the course of my life
And that God was not around
I searched for Him both night and day
God's peace could not be found

I heard the voice of Jesus say
If you don't forgive, I will not forgive you
I suffered, bled, died on the cross
For all the sins that you do

Unforgiveness only burdens you down
And God wants you to be free
Jesus purchased our Salvation
On the cross of Calvary

Know that God has given you a decision to make
He will not control what you must do
His commands say forgive one another
On Calvary's cross He did it for you

Wake-Up Call

This is a wake-up call
For those who are left behind
There is an appointed day for you, my friend
It could come at any moment, any time

Jesus has given many chances
Many doors have been opened for you
He has paid the high cost for your salvation
What in the world are you going to do?

You must confess all your sins to Jesus
There must be a complete change in your life
He will work in the depths of your dark heart
To remove all bitterness, envy, hatred, and strife

He will replace it with love in your heart
A surrendered life is what you must give
Committing your all to the Lord Jesus Christ
Then in heaven one day you will live

We Are All On Our Way

We are all on our way to meet Jesus
We must all go through the grave
When He calls your name on that appointed day
Tell me, what in the world are you going to say?

We are all on our way to meet Jesus
He will find all the work that you have done
Will He say, Faithful servant, you've done very well
On earth you glorified My Son

We are all on our way to meet Jesus
Salvation has always been free
There is a heaven and a hell
One has been reserved just for you and me

Why Do I Make You So Small, God?

Why do I make You, God, so small?
When You control the heavens above
I look at the stars up in the sky
They display Your perfect love

You uphold the heavens
In the palm of Your hand
And evidence of Your doing
Are displayed upon all the land

Why do I make You so small, God?
I know this is sin for me
For I become anxious
Spiritual things I cannot see

So, I confess my sin before You
For You are big and not small
And yet You love even me
You are concerned about my all

Valley of Encouragement

In our pain and suffering, we choose not to grumble or mumble; instead we choose to look to the cross, the high price Jesus paid for our sins that we might have eternal life. Yes, pain is real, devastating, and debilitating at times, but we are overcomers by the blood of the Lamb (Rev. 12:11). God had commanded them not to eat of this tree, but they could eat of any other tree in the garden. They disobeyed God. He has given us the Holy Ghost and His Spirit lives inside of you. He keeps you and brings healing, peace, and comfort. Your mission is to trust the Lord in the Valley of Encouragement, for He will bring you out with joy.

As we walk through this valley, we choose to encourage others. We choose not to focus on the negative things in life. We choose to find a flower in the desert. In the Word of God, He tells us to bring every thought captive. The Scripture says, "Casting down imaginations, and every high thing that exalteth itself against the knowledge of God, and bringing into captivity every thought to the obedience of Christ..." (2 Cor. 10:5). Paul tells us in Philippians 4:8 to "think on these things, whatsoever things are true, whatsoever thing are honest, whatsoever things are just, whatsoever things are pure, whatsoever things are lovely, whatsoever things are of good report; if there be any virtue, if there be any praise think on these things".

A Servant's Clothes

A servant of the Lord
Is what I want to be
Clothed in His righteousness
And His humility

Being led by the Spirit
Walking in His power and might
Praying for the children of God
Morning, noon, and night

A servant who is yielded
And learning to be still
Who has completely surrendered
To the Father's will

Walking not by sight
I will trust and obey
Seeking God for daily guidance
Down the straight and narrow way

Accepted

The need to be accepted
For someone to really see
To be treasured as a person
That there's value within me

The need to be encouraged
Expelling doubts and fears
To help build my self-esteem
That's been damaged for so many years

The need for self-expression
To learn from others as I grow
To share the love of God
Even with people I don't know

The need for a special friend
Lord, you've been that friend to me
There is nothing in the whole wide world
That can replace my love for Thee

Broken But Useable

No one wants to be broken
No one wants to be flawed
But I am here to tell you
This is how you must present yourself to God

He doesn't need you to be perfect
As the world implies that you must be
He doesn't need all of your learning
But He requires humility

He wants you to throw yourself
Upon Jesus, the cornerstone
So that He can break you and make you again
He will shape you for His very own

You will be broken but useable
He will place His Spirit in your heart
With scars of suffering and pain
But His Spirit of grace shall not depart

Dark Night of the Soul

This is a dark night of the soul
You feel that God has abandoned you
You have cried out in prayer
Not knowing what else to do

You want to hear His voice
Or even just a touch
The silence is just killing you
Are you asking for too much?

Negative thoughts invade your mind
And you're wondering what you have done
Have you sinned or said something
That was harmful to someone?

You want the Lord to cleanse you
From whatever lurks inside
You eagerly want to confess it
You want His peace to abide

It's a dark night of the soul
You must trust that He is there
Silence is a lesson to learn
His grace and mercy He will always share

So, let Him have His way with you
There is a purpose and a healing inside
For in your pain and suffering
Let the Savior be glorified

Go the Extra Mile

Give above and beyond what is expected of you
Always go the extra mile
Give and it shall be given unto you
Try to lift someone's spirit, make them smile

No, it is not your duty
But your heart says yes, I care
Just a little bit of your time
Can let someone know you are there

Our world is about making money
Cut corners wherever you can
But God is watching you when no one sees
He will judge the works of every man

So, let's get back to basics
Let the change begin with you
Help your brother or sister or fellow man
God will bless the things that you do

He Leads The Way

We saw you when you grabbed her hand
And tenderly led the way
When they had the call to worship
And you both knelt down to pray

You petitioned the Lord above
To cleanse your heart from any sin
I know you ask Him to cover your children
For the Holy Spirit to abide within

We saw Christ's love overflowing
And His light shone upon your face
The Holy Spirit's indwelling
We see you are covered with His grace

In His Presence

Just to stand, Lord, in your presence
I humbly bow and praise your name
You have changed my life forever
I will never ever be the same

He changed me from the inside out
I will never ever be the same
I give glory and honor to Jesus
He cleansed my sin and shame

For now, I belong to Jesus
I am content wherever He leads
He will protect and give me peace
The Holy Spirit guides me faithfully

Jesus Loves Even Me

I am overwhelmed by the fact
That Jesus could love even me
And He thought that I was worth it
He came and died on Calvary

He said that I was His child
That I was His very own
That He would never leave or forsake me
It's by grace His love is shown

He said He redeemed me by His blood
He has washed me, I am white as snow
And now, I can sing the wonderful song
Jesus loves me, this I know

One day I will go home with Him
I will confess my sin and shame
He gave me the gift of salvation
And I have never been the same

Journey to the Crown

We are blessed beyond measure
God's faithfulness is true
Although you can't find your way out
This journey is prepared for you

He knows the way that you must go
He will lead and guide the way
You must learn to trust the Lord your God
And seek His face, child, everyday

There is a crown of righteousness
That God alone has prepared
Trust Him on this journey of faith
A golden crown He will give you up there

Joy

I love to see the joy and smile upon your face
I love to see the enthusiasm
As you talk about God's saving grace
I love the Word of God
Expressions that you give
It makes us want to read it more
And apply His Word to how to live
It makes us want more of Him
Jesus Christ, our Lord
And receive the wonderful blessings
And new life that He restores

Man of God

My son, you are a man of God
May His Spirit rest on you
I pray that you would seek Him daily
For the things that you must do

You are called to help God's people
You are a leader that He can use
He has a purpose for your life, young man
It's a call you cannot refuse

You must spend time in His Word
It's the most important thing He has called you to do
Surrender your will to Jesus
For He will continue to change you

God will open up doors for you
Faith and trust will pave the way
Humility and integrity will cover you
As you seek the Lord God each day

Suffer the Children

God holds us responsible
For He loves the children so
From generation to generation
He holds us accountable, don't you know?

Where are the children? God asks
Suffer them to come unto me
Teach, train and love them
In the things that bring glory

Let your attitude towards children
Be consistent, show them you care
Teach them God's moral standards
That they might use everywhere

The Influence of a Mother

On this Mother's Day
I want to encourage you
Stay strong with your principles
On the things you say and do

This world has a great influence
On our children everyday
They are trying to change their thinking
For humanism is taught in some kind of way

We used to share the Word of God
And church played an important part
We taught them the Word of God
For safekeeping in their hearts

We have given them too much power
To make decisions they should never have
Now they have no respect for you
It's really quite very sad

Prisons are full of our children
This should never be
The streets and drugs have claimed them
They lack responsibility

So, I encourage you, dear Mothers
How are you living your life today?
Is God the center of your focus?
What does your life display?

You Are God's Light

You are God's light in a darkened world
Like a city that sits on a hill
You have got to know your purpose
Daily, you must surrender your will

It's not what you go through but how
It's the attitude where your character is made
You are on display for many to see
Let the negative thoughts simply fade

Let the joy of the Lord exude from you
With God's inner peace inside
That no matter what comes and goes in your life
His presence and His Spirit abide

About the Author

Carolyn Stovall was the first of four children born to Bettye and Calvin Rodgers in Lincoln, Nebraska. Carolyn has been married to retired SMSGT Ted Stovall for forty-six years and they have two daughters, Brooke Awan and Sarah Alvarado-Vallejo. They also have five grandchildren who are their hearts' joy, Noah, Caleb, Faith, Seth, and Solomon, and a great grandson, Malachi.

She received her spiritual training at an early age through her grandmother Sarah Tarpley. Her life-long passion for community service is the result of the impact the church made on her early life.

Carolyn has a B.A. in Psychology and Sociology and a minor in Women's Studies from Bellevue College (Bellevue, Nebraska). She also has a Master's in Community Counseling from St. Mary's University (San

Antonio, Texas). Carolyn has worked and served in San Antonio as a Psychotherapist and is retired.

Carolyn Stovall has volunteered in churches and communities everywhere her family was stationed. She currently volunteers at Brook Army Medical Center. Regarding her work, Carolyn says, "There are so many people with special needs, so many tasks, and too few people to do them. I feel I have been blessed, so to sacrifice my time and talent is the least I can do to spread Christ's love to a hurting world." Carolyn has let nothing stop her from ministering to God's people. She has had a bout with cancer and has severe back pain; but God gives her the strength she needs to accomplish great things for His glory.

Carolyn is a member of Lackland Air Force Base Permanent Party Chapel and attends its Gospel Service, where she taught Bible studies for twenty-four years and is a member of the Gospel Choir. She has also been a guest speaker at many churches and Women's Retreats around the country, where she has also shared her gift of poetry. Carolyn's first book of poetry, Psalms of Life, has given many comfort and strength.

CPSIA information can be obtained
at www.ICGtesting.com
Printed in the USA
LVHW041916151220
674244LV00017BA/2622

9 781632 216397